Sensei Self Development

Mental Health Chronicles Series

Recognizing and Managing Negative Thought Patterns

Sensei Paul David

Copyright Page

Sensei Self Development -
Recognizing and Managing Negative Thought Patterns,
by Sensei Paul David

Copyright © 2024

All rights reserved.

978-1-77848-317-2 SSD_Journals_Amazon_PaperbackBook_Recognizing and Managing Negative Thought Patterns

978-1-77848-316-5
SSD_Journals_Amazon_eBook_Recognizing and Managing Negative Thought Patterns

978-1-77848-445-2
SSD_Journals_Ingram_Paperback_Recognizing and Managing Negative Thought

This book is not authorized for free distribution copying.

www.senseipublishing.com

@senseipublishing
#senseipublishing

Get/Share Your FREE SSD Mental Health Chronicles at
www.senseiselfdevelopment.care

or

CLICK HERE

Check Out The SSD Chronicles Series CLICK HERE

Dedication

To those who courageously take action towards self-improvement - you are helping to evolve the world for generations to come.

- It's a great day to be alive!

If Found Please Contact:

_____

Reward If Found:

_____

MY COMMITMENT

I, _____ commit to writing This Sensei Self Development Journal for at least 10 days in a row, starting: _____

Writing this journal is valuable to me because:

_____
_____
_____
_____
_____

If I finish a minimum of 10 consecutive days of writing in this journal, I will reward myself by:

_____
_____
_____
_____

_____

_____

If I don't finish 10 days of writing this journal, I will promise to:

_____

_____

_____

_____

_____

I will do the following things to ensure that I write in my Sensei Self Development Journal every day:

_____

_____

_____

_____

_____

Get/Share Your FREE All-Ages Mental Health eBook Now at
www.senseiselfdevelopment.com
Or CLICK HERE

senseiselfdevelopment.com

Check Out Another Book In The
SSD BOOK SERIES:
senseipublishing.com/SSD_SERIES
CLICK HERE

Join Our Publishing Journey!

If you would like to receive FUTURE FREE BOOKS and get to know us better, please click www.senseipublishing.com and join our newsletter by entering your email address in the pop-up box.

Follow Our Blog: senseipauldavid.ca

Follow/Like/Subscribe: Facebook, Instagram, YouTube: @senseipublishing

Scan the QR Code with your phone or tablet
to follow us on social media: Like / Subscribe / Follow

A Message From The Author:
Sensei Paul David

Dear Reader,

Welcome to the world of mental health journaling – a sacred space for self-reflection, growth, and healing. Within these pages, you hold the power to uplift your spirit, invigorate your mind, and nourish your goals.

In a world that often moves at blink-and-you'll-miss-it speed, it's crucial to make time for self-care and self-discovery.

Anxiety, stress, and emotional turbulence may have clouded your mind, making it difficult to find clarity and peace within. But fear not! Together, we will navigate the labyrinth of emotions, and experiences, helping to simplify the path to mental well-being.

This journal is not merely a bunch of blank pages awaiting your words. It is your compassionate companion, offering solace and understanding during your unique journey. Here, you are free to unburden yourself, celebrate small and large victories, and confront the challenges that may still linger.

Within the sheltered realm of these pages, there is no judgment, no expectation, and no pressure. Your unique experience and perspective hold immeasurable worth, and your voice deserves to be heard. Whether you choose to fill the lines with eloquence or simply scribble fragments of your thoughts, please remember each entry is a valuable contribution to your growth.

In this sacred space, you are challenged to take off the mask we so often wear in the outside world. It is here that you can be raw, vulnerable, and authentic – allowing your true self to be seen and embraced without reservation. By giving yourself permission to explore the depths of your emotions and confront the shadows that may lurk within, you will discover profound insights and find the healing you seek over time.

As you embark on this journaling journey, I encourage you to embrace the process itself rather than fixate solely on the outcome. Remember, it is not about reaching a certain destination or ticking off boxes on a list of accomplishments. Rather, it is about cultivating self-awareness, fostering self-compassion, and nurturing a sense of curiosity about the intricate workings of your intelligently beautiful mind.

In the quiet moments of reflection, let your pen become a bridge between your inner world and the possibilities that lie ahead. Create a sanctuary for your thoughts, fears, triumphs, and dreams. As you pour your heart onto these pages, allow your words to be a living testament to courage, resilience, and an unwavering commitment to your own well-being.

I am honored to be a part of your journey, and I believe in your ability to navigate the twists and turns with grace and resilience. Remember, you are not alone in this – countless others have walked similar paths, faced similar challenges, and emerged stronger and wiser on the other side. You have the power to reclaim all of your untapped joy, cultivate a positive mindset that serves you, and foster a deep sense of self-love and peaceful confident. – And it will take a worth effort and time.

So, open the first page of this journal with hope, curiosity, and an open heart and open mind. Embrace the transformative power of self-reflection, and allow it to guide you towards a life of greater fulfilment and peace. Each journaling session is an opportunity to not only connect with yourself but also to rekindle the light within that sometimes flickers but never extinguishes.

Remember, the pages you are about to fill are not just a record of your journey but also a testament to your strength, resilience, and indomitable spirit. Cherish this space, invest in yourself, and let your words be an ode to the magnificent journey of becoming whole.

With great respect for your decision to evolve,

Paul

MY CONVICTION

Please circle your answers below

I am DECIDING to be patient with myself and this PROCESS each time I journal toward my improved state of mental well-being

        YES   NO

"The present moment is filled with joy and happiness. If you are attentive, you will see it."

Thich Nhat Hanh

Introduction

Back in the 1960s, Aaron Beck brought a big change to psychotherapy with his development of Cognitive Behavior Therapy (CBT), which he first called cognitive therapy. Beck noticed that many of his patients with depression had thoughts that weren't exactly true and were full of what he called "cognitive distortions." This observation led him to see depression as more of a thinking problem than just a mood issue. His influential work, especially his 1979 book "Cognitive Therapy for Depression," really changed the way we understand depression.

Since then, CBT has been researched a lot and has proven to be effective for various psychiatric disorders like depression, anxiety, eating disorders, substance abuse, and personality disorders. It's also really useful alongside medication for treating tougher conditions like bipolar disorder and schizophrenia. What's great about CBT is its flexibility; it's been adapted for different groups, including children, teenagers, adults, couples, and families. It's not just for mental health issues, either; it's been effective for nonpsychiatric problems like irritable bowel syndrome, chronic fatigue syndrome, fibromyalgia, insomnia, migraines, and chronic pain.

At the heart of CBT is a key idea: negative thought patterns

Negative thought patterns, or cognitive distortions, are irrational or extreme ways of thinking that can skew how we see the world. They often lead to a more negative outlook, heighten emotional struggles, and can contribute to mental health problems like anxiety and depression. Let's look at some common cognitive distortions and examples of them:

1. All-or-Nothing Thinking (Black-and-White Thinking):This involves seeing things in only two categories without recognizing any middle ground. Example: "If I'm not perfect at this task, then I'm a total failure."

2. Overgeneralization: This is making broad interpretations from a single or few events. Example: "I didn't get the job. I'll never get any job."

3. Mental Filtering: This involves focusing exclusively on the negatives and ignoring

the positives. Example: "My presentation was terrible because I stuttered once."

Whenever I describe negative thought patterns, a bulb of recognition lights up in people's mind. These thought patterns are so prevalent that virtually everyone experiences them. But despite being everywhere, they go unnoticed and unchallenged, like microbes that surround us. It's time for you to wake up and start standing up to them.

The metaphor for standing up is apt because this is how these thought patterns can be dealt with: by being identified, confronted and then replaced – again and again. Until they remain a shadow of themselves. Too weak to cause harm.

Here's how that confrontation looks like:

It begins with identifying these thoughts, which are often exaggerated or irrational beliefs like "I always fail" or "No one likes me." It's important to pinpoint these thoughts because they usually fuel feelings of anxiety, sadness, or low self-esteem.

The next step is challenging these thoughts. This involves critically examining their truth and considering more rational, realistic alternatives. It's about questioning the accuracy of these negative beliefs and testing whether they hold up under scrutiny. For instance, if you think "I always fail," you'd look for instances where you've succeeded or done well, which contradicts this belief.

Finally, the process involves reframing these thoughts into more positive and realistic ones. This isn't about forcing yourself to be relentlessly positive; it's about finding a more balanced, fair perspective. An example would be changing a thought like "I'll never be good at this" to something more rational, such as "I may not be perfect, but I can improve with practice." This step is crucial as it helps shift your mindset from a negative, defeating outlook to one that's more empowering and grounded in reality.

By following these steps, CBT aims to transform the way you think, gradually leading to more positive emotions and healthier behaviors.

Here are two examples of this process in action:

A Student Facing Academic Failure:
- Situation: The student fails a test.
- Thought: "I'm a failure and I'm never going to succeed."

- Feeling: This thought spirals into feelings of worthlessness and depression.
- Behavior: Consequently, the student might start avoiding studying or attending classes, thinking it won't make a difference.
- CBT Intervention: The therapist helps the student to see this situation differently. They work together to reshape the thought into something like, "This test was hard, but one test doesn't define my entire academic ability. I can learn from this experience and improve."

Dealing with Social Anxiety:

- Situation: An individual with social anxiety is invited to a party.
- Thought: "I'll say something stupid and everyone will laugh at me."
- Feeling: This worry leads to intense anxiety and fear.
- Behavior: The person decides to skip the party to avoid these uncomfortable feelings.
- CBT Intervention: Here, the therapist collaborates with the individual to break down and understand these fears.

Together, they develop strategies for coping with anxiety. The individual is encouraged to gradually face social situations, helping them realize that their fears are often exaggerated and that they can manage social interactions more effectively than they thought.

The Connection Between Negative Thought Patterns and Depression

The connection between negative thought patterns and depression is quite direct and significant. When someone is experiencing depression, they often fall into negative thinking patterns. These aren't just occasional negative thoughts; they are persistent and deeply rooted, affecting how the person views themselves, their future, and the world around them.

This relationship is like a two-way street. On one hand, depression can make a person more prone to negative thinking. On the other hand, these negative thoughts can deepen and prolong the depression. It's a cycle that feeds into itself. For example, someone with depression might constantly think they're not good enough or that things will never get better. These thoughts reinforce the feelings of sadness and hopelessness that are central to depression.

Breaking this cycle is key in dealing with depression. That's why a lot of treatments for depression, like cognitive-behavioral therapy, focus on changing these negative thought patterns. The idea is to challenge and replace them with more balanced and realistic thoughts. This can help lighten the mood and reduce depressive symptoms.

List of Negative Thought Patterns

Dealing with cognitive distortions is a central part of Cognitive Behavioral Therapy (CBT), and the most crucial step in this process is identifying these distortions. Think of these negative thoughts as faulty programming in your mind, like bugs in a system, causing feelings like anxiety or depression.

The task at hand is to recognize these flawed patterns and then work on rewriting them. This process is gradual because these patterns are often deeply ingrained, having developed over years or even decades. It's a bit like chipping away at a large block; you remove a small piece at a time.

An instance of rewriting these thoughts, however, can be relatively quick. It involves reframing, a technique where you challenge and change your immediate negative thoughts to more balanced ones. For example, if you spill tea and think, "I'm so clumsy," you quickly counter that with, "Spilling tea sometimes doesn't make me clumsy. I do many things carefully every day." This shift in perspective takes just a few seconds.

Knowing these common negative thought patterns is beneficial. Once you're familiar with them, you'll start noticing them more often in your daily life and hence be able to change them. We will go through the most common distortions one by one. While going through them, try to reflect on moments in your life where you may have fallen into these patterns of thinking

1. All-or-nothing thinking: This is where you see things in black or white categories. If a situation falls short of perfect, you see it as a total failure. For instance, you might feel like you're a terrible cook because one dish didn't turn out as expected, ignoring the many times you've successfully prepared meals. To counter this, remind yourself that most aspects of life exist in

shades of gray and that a single shortcoming doesn't define your overall ability.

2. Overgeneralization: You see a single negative event as a never-ending pattern of defeat. For example, if you didn't get a job you interviewed for, you might think, "I'll never get a job." However, one rejection doesn't predict future failures. It's important to recognize that each opportunity is different and that past outcomes don't dictate future ones.

3. Mental Filtering: This involves picking out a single negative detail and dwelling on it exclusively. Imagine you gave a presentation and one person criticized it, leading you to forget the positive feedback from others. To combat this, try to view situations more holistically and acknowledge both positive and negative aspects.

4. Discounting the Positive: You reject positive experiences by insisting they "don't count." If you do well on a task, you might think that it was just luck. To counteract this distortion, practice accepting compliments and positive results as valid and reflective of your abilities.

5. Jumping to Conclusions: This includes mind-reading (assuming the thoughts and intentions of others) and fortune telling (predicting how

things will turn out). For example, thinking a friend didn't text back because they're angry with you, or assuming a presentation will go poorly before it happens. It's crucial to remind yourself that you cannot read minds or predict the future, and to check the facts before drawing conclusions.

6. Magnification (Catastrophizing) or Minimization: This involves blowing things out of proportion or inappropriately shrinking their importance. For instance, magnifying a mistake you made while minimizing your successes. It's helpful to keep a balanced perspective and evaluate situations based on all evidence, not just the negative aspects.

7. Emotional Reasoning: You believe that what you feel must be true automatically. If you feel stupid, you believe you must be stupid. To dispute this, remind yourself that feelings are not facts and that emotions can be based on misperceptions.

8. Should Statements: You try to motivate yourself with "shoulds" and "shouldn'ts," as if you need to be punished before you can expect to do anything. For example, thinking "I should never make mistakes" can lead to frustration. Instead, replace "should" with "would like to,"

which is less about guilt and more about preference.

9. Labeling and Mislabeling: This involves describing an event or yourself with a highly colored and emotionally loaded term. For example, instead of saying you made a mistake, you label yourself an "idiot." To counter this, describe the situation in more neutral, factual terms.

10. Personalization: This means assuming responsibility for a negative event when there was no direct involvement. For example, thinking a friend's mood is due to something you did. To dispute this, consider other factors that may have influenced the situation and remember that not everything is about you or within your control.

Recognizing these patterns in your thinking can help you start to question and challenge them, leading to more balanced and rational thought processes.

How to Deal With Negative Thought Patterns

There are many ways of dealing with negative thought patterns. Although you won't need to use each one of the strategies given below, you will need many of them. Just like a mechanic needs many tools to fix a problem, you also need multiple tools to deal with negative thought patterns. Some strategies will work better in one situation, and at one time, than the other (Don't worry about it; you will know). And some strategies will work better for you personally just like some foods taste better to you. Your job is to taste different strategies and then create a diet that is best for you. My diet mostly consists of CBT, Self-compassion, and sidestepping thoughts. Yours could look different.

Cognitive Behavioral Therapy:

1. Recognize Negative Thoughts: Start by identifying your negative thoughts. Pay attention to moments when you feel anxious, depressed, or upset and write down the thoughts that are going through your mind.

2. Challenge These Thoughts: Once you've identified a negative thought, challenge it. Ask yourself questions like: "Is this thought based on facts or my assumptions? What evidence do I have for and against this thought? Is there a more positive or realistic way of looking at the situation?"

3. Reframe Your Thoughts: Replace negative or unrealistic thoughts with more positive, realistic ones. For example, change "I always fail" to "Sometimes I succeed, sometimes I don't, but I can learn from my mistakes."

4. Behavioral Experiments (optional): Test out the validity of your negative thoughts through behavioral experiments. For instance, if you think "No one likes me," try initiating a conversation and observe the outcome.

Remember, while self-guided CBT techniques can be effective for managing mild to moderate negative thoughts, seeking professional help is advisable if you're dealing with severe anxiety, depression, or other mental health conditions.

Self-Compassion

One way to disarm negative thought patterns is Self-compassion. Self-compassion is about treating yourself with the same kindness and understanding that you would offer to a close friend in a similar situation. When negative thoughts and self-criticism surface, self-compassion steps in as a soothing voice, reminding you that it's okay to be imperfect and experience difficulties.

The practice of self-compassion directly addresses the harshness of negative thoughts.

For example, if you catch yourself thinking, "I'm such a failure for making that mistake," self-compassion changes this narrative to something more nurturing like, "Everyone makes mistakes, and that's okay. I can learn from this and move forward." This shift in mindset can significantly reduce the intensity and frequency of negative thoughts.

By regularly practicing self-compassion, you create a kinder internal dialogue. Over time, this practice will lead to a more balanced and positive outlook on life, enhancing overall well-being.

Self-compassion offers a distinct approach compared to Cognitive Behavioral Therapy (CBT), which typically involves challenging the accuracy of our negative thoughts. In CBT, you might confront a thought like, "You think I'm clumsy?" by countering it with evidence to the contrary, proving to yourself that you're not clumsy. While this method is effective, self-compassion takes a different route. It involves responding with understanding and acceptance, saying, "It's okay to be clumsy. Everyone has their moments." This approach doesn't argue with the thought but instead offers kindness and empathy towards oneself, acknowledging that it's normal to have imperfections.

Here is how you can practice self-compassion:

1. Self-Kindness: Replace self-criticism with self-kindness. When you notice you're being hard on yourself, pause and ask, "Would I say this to a good friend?" If the answer is no, reframe your thoughts to be more compassionate and supportive, as you would to a friend.

2. Common Humanity: Remind yourself that you're not alone in your struggles. Everyone experiences setbacks, failures, and imperfections. Recognizing this can help you feel more connected to others and less isolated in your difficulties.

3. Comforting Physical Gestures: Simple physical gestures can promote self-compassion. For instance, placing a hand over your heart or giving yourself a gentle hug can be soothing and serve as a physical reminder to treat yourself with care and understanding.

4. Positive Self-Talk: Develop a habit of positive self-talk. This involves speaking to yourself in a kind, encouraging tone, especially during challenging times.

> Replace harsh or critical thoughts with affirmations or statements that acknowledge your worth and strengths.

Each of these can be categorised as a strategy on its own. So consider them four strategies instead of one. They are all very effective.

Change Your Beliefs

Negative thought patterns are often rooted in deep-seated beliefs about ourselves and the world around us. These beliefs can shape our perceptions, influencing how we interpret experiences and interactions. For instance, a belief like "I am not good enough" can lead to constant self-criticism, while a belief such as "The world is a dangerous place" might result in excessive worry or avoidance behaviors.

Changing these beliefs is key to transforming negative thought patterns. This process starts with identifying both the self-related beliefs and the beliefs about the world that are feeding into your negativity. For example, alongside a personal belief of inadequacy, you might also hold the belief that "people can't be trusted" or "success is impossible in today's world."

Once these beliefs are identified, the next step is to challenge and reevaluate them. This involves looking at the evidence that supports or contradicts these beliefs. For personal beliefs, recall instances of personal strength, achievement, or resilience. For beliefs about the world, seek out stories and examples that demonstrate kindness, success, and safety.

Practicing affirmations can help in reshaping both sets of beliefs. Create affirmations that address both personal self-worth and a more positive view of the world. Statements like "I am capable and deserving of success" and "There is goodness and opportunity in the world" can be effective.

Visualization can also be used to challenge and change these beliefs. Imagine scenarios where you feel competent and valued, and visualize the world as a place of opportunity and positivity. This mental practice can gradually start to shift your internal narrative.

Engaging in behavioral experiments is another practical way to challenge these beliefs. By putting yourself in situations that counter your negative beliefs and observing the outcomes, you can gather real-life evidence that challenges these perceptions. For instance, engaging in a new social setting or taking on a challenging project can provide counter-evidence to beliefs of personal inadequacy or a hostile world.

Changing deep-seated beliefs about oneself and the world takes time and consistent effort. However, by methodically challenging these beliefs and reinforcing positive perspectives, you can gradually transform your thought patterns, leading to improved mental health and a more balanced outlook on life.

Slowww It Dowwn!

Reminding yourself to slow down mentally is a crucial step in managing stress and improving overall well-being. In our fast-paced environment, where multitasking and constant busyness are often the norm, our minds tend to race from one thought to another, leading to a state of mental exhaustion. By consciously reminding ourselves to slow down, we can create a much-needed space for rest and clarity.

Start by setting small, regular reminders throughout your day. It could be a note on your desk, an alarm on your phone, or even a specific routine, like pausing for a moment each time you have a cup of coffee. These reminders serve as prompts to take a brief mental break. During these breaks, focus on simple activities that bring your attention to the present moment, such as observing your surroundings, feeling the texture of an object, or listening to the sounds around you.

Incorporating deep breathing exercises can also be a powerful tool in slowing down your mind. When you notice your thoughts racing, take a few deep breaths. With each inhale and exhale, allow your mind to focus solely on your breathing, letting other thoughts pass by without engagement. This helps in reducing the immediacy of stressful thoughts and brings a sense of calm to your mind.

Another aspect of slowing down is learning to recognize when your thoughts are unnecessarily speeding up. Often, our minds get caught up in hypothetical scenarios or replay past events. When you catch yourself in these patterns, gently remind yourself to return to the present. It's about acknowledging the rush of thoughts and then choosing to step back, to view them with a sense of detachment and calm.

Changing Habits of Mind that Lead to Negative Thought Patterns

One way to deal with negative thoughts is to face them squarely, like you're stepping the into a fight. Another way is just to stay home, away from it all, meaning not engage with your thoughts at all. The less you're out dealing with the world's scammers, thieves, and liars, the less stressed you'll likely be. Similarly, less you will engage with obviously false negative thoughts you are engaged, the less likely you will feel stressed. Sure, we all need to get out for work or some fun, but we don't have to be out there all the time, getting lost in the mind's chaos.

Say you're on vacation with your family and negative thoughts start creeping in. That's not the time to dive into heavy stuff like CBT. What you can do instead is just unplug. Tell yourself, "Nah, forget that. I'm not going to worry about it now. Let's just have fun." The idea is to completely step away from overthinking and negativity. Just let it go and enjoy the moment. Disengage. Disengage.

1. Overthinking:

While it's beneficial to be thoughtful, overanalyzing every decision can be a trap. For instance, if choosing where to eat lunch becomes a struggle filled with insecurity and doubt, you're likely overthinking. This habit involves examining every angle of a decision and trying to predict every outcome, which can be mentally exhausting and distressing, especially when things don't turn out as expected. To combat this, set time limits for decision-making and adhere to them. Try to catch yourself overthinking a) an event b) or a decision, and disengage.

If you are suffering from indecision at any given moment, just do the right thing you know intuitively or choose the option that would minimise regret.

2. Rumination:

Self-reflection is important, but when it's tainted with constant negativity and a focus on personal faults, it turns into harmful rumination. This habit involves a repetitive cycle where you dwell on your flaws and past mistakes, leading to a bleak outlook on the future. To break free from this pattern, actively engage in different activities when you notice these thoughts arising. Reading, watching a movie, pursuing a hobby, or spending time with friends can be helpful. However, it's crucial to avoid using friends just to vent negative thoughts, and to steer clear of food and alcohol as distractions, as they may exacerbate the problem.

Avoiding overthinking and rumination works even better to combat negative thought patterns if you are someone who thinks and ruminates a lot, like I tend to do. A lot of the time, rather than getting into back and forth with my thoughts, I just sidestep them.

The best strategy is a combination of confrontation (CBT, self compassion, etc) and sidestepping. The ratio will depend on how you think. Try different strategies and find the protocol that works best for you.

Schedule Time for Negative Thinking

Scheduling your negative thinking is a unique strategy to manage negative thought patterns. It involves deliberately allocating a specific time each day to focus on and process these thoughts. This approach may sound unusual, but it can be quite effective in compartmentalizing negative feelings and preventing them from overwhelming your day. Here's how to implement this technique:

1. Set a Specific Time: Choose a 10- or 15-minute block each day for your negative thinking. It could be a time when you are least likely to be interrupted, like early morning or during a mid-afternoon break.

2. Create a Negative Thought Journal: Keep a journal dedicated to this practice. During your allocated time, write down all the negative thoughts that come to mind. This can include worries, fears, frustrations, or any recurring negative thoughts.

3. Focused Negative Thinking: During your scheduled time, allow yourself to fully experience and acknowledge these negative thoughts and feelings. The goal is not to judge or change these thoughts but to simply let them exist.

4. Closure: When your time is up, close your journal and move on with your day. This act symbolizes leaving these negative thoughts in the journal and not carrying them with you.

5. Reflect and Evaluate: Occasionally, look back through your journal to reflect on your thoughts. Over time, you may notice patterns or triggers for your negative thinking, which can be insightful for further personal growth.

6. Balance with Positivity: Balance this practice with positive activities or thoughts. Following your negative thinking session, engage in something uplifting, like a brief walk, listening to your favorite song, or a short meditation.

By scheduling time for negative thinking and confining it to a specific part of your day, you can prevent these thoughts from dominating your entire day. This method offers a structured way to acknowledge and understand your negative emotions without letting them control your life.

Journaling

Journaling can be a powerful tool in dealing with negative thought patterns. Journaling is usually paired with other strategies such as CBT and self compassion. Or it can be used on its own as a mode to release pent up unprocessed emotions and events.

Journaling involves writing down your thoughts and feelings, which can help you process and understand them better. Here's how journaling can be used effectively:

1. Awareness: Journaling brings awareness to your negative thought patterns. When you write down your thoughts, it's easier to see patterns and triggers that you might not notice otherwise.

2. Reflection: It allows for reflection. You can look back at what you've written and see how your thoughts and fee evolved over time. This

can provide insight into how certain situations or emotions affect you.

3. Reframing Thoughts: Writing in a journal offers a chance to reframe negative thoughts. For example, you can challenge a thought like, "I'm always unsuccessful," by writing about times you have succeeded or made progress.

4. Emotional Release: Journaling provides a safe, private space to express and release emotions. This can be especially helpful if you find it hard to talk about your feelings with others.

5. Positive Reinforcement: You can also use journaling to reinforce positive thoughts and experiences. Writing about things you're grateful for or achievements you're proud of can help balance the negative thoughts.

6. Tracking Progress: Over time, journaling can help you track your progress in managing negative thoughts. You can see how your coping strategies have evolved and how your mindset has changed.

7. Identifying Triggers: Regular journaling can help you identify triggers that lead to negative thought patterns. Once you're aware of these triggers, you can develop strategies to deal with them more effectively.

Incorporating journaling into your daily routine can be a simple yet effective way to manage and understand your thought patterns, contributing to better mental health and well-being.

***

Here is my, Sensei Paul's, Mantra for dealing with Negative Thoughts or Thought Patterns:

1. Process
2. Disengage
3. Distract

First, I engage with the thought using CBT, self compassion, journaling, or just plain thinking (there are many more ways you can try – anything that involves engaging with the thought constructively.)

Once I have come to a conclusion, I must disengage, meaning not entertain it again and again. It's like telling your thought, "we already discussed this issue once".

Once that is done, I "distract" myself, which means doing something productive, because an empty mind is a devil's workshop.

Before We Get Started...

Remember, mindfulness journaling is a personal practice, and these questions are meant to guide and inspire you. Feel free to adapt and modify them to suit your needs and preferences. Explore, reflect, and embrace the opportunity to deepen your self-awareness and cultivate a sense of inner peace.

Date ___/___/___ : S M T W Th F S

I feel:
(please circle)

because _____ because _____ because _____ because _____ because _____

Today I Am Grateful For
1. _____
2. _____
3. _____

What could help transform today into a remarkable day?

Reflective Writing

How does the recognition and management of negative thought patterns help to improve my mental health?

_____
_____
_____
_____
_____
_____
_____

Which of the following is an example of a negative thought pattern?

A) "I can do this."
B) "I always make mistakes."
C) "I am a hard worker."
D) "I am proud of my accomplishments."

All Are Correct - Choose The Response You Feel Is Most Important To Remember

Date ___/___/___ : S M T W Th F S

I feel:
(please circle)

🙂	😁	😋	😞	😠
because	because	because	because	because
_____	_____	_____	_____	_____

Today I Am Grateful For
1. _____
2. _____
3. _____

What could help transform today into a remarkable day?

Reflective Writing

What strategies can I use to become aware of my negative thought patterns?

_____
_____
_____
_____
_____
_____
_____

Which cognitive distortion is characterized by seeing things as either all good or all bad?

A) Overgeneralization
B) Polarized thinking
C) Personalization
D) Catastrophizing

All Are Correct - Choose The Response You Feel Is Most Important To Remember

Date ___/___/___ : S M T W Th F S

I feel:
(please circle)

because _____ because _____ because _____ because _____ because _____

Today I Am Grateful For
1. _____
2. _____
3. _____

What could help transform today into a remarkable day?

Reflective Writing
What techniques can I use to challenge my negative thinking?

_____
_____
_____
_____
_____
_____
_____

Which of the following is an effective strategy for managing negative thought patterns?

A) Ignoring negative thoughts
B) Dwelling on negative thoughts
C) Engaging in positive self-talk
D) Avoiding challenging situations

All Are Correct - Choose The Response You Feel Is Most Important To Remember

Date ___/___/___ : S M T W Th F S

I feel:
(please circle)

because _____ because _____ because _____ because _____ because _____

Today I Am Grateful For
1. _____
2. _____
3. _____

What could help transform today into a remarkable day?

Reflective Writing

How can I use affirmations to replace my negative thinking?

_____
_____
_____
_____
_____
_____
_____

"I will never be successful" is an example of which cognitive distortion?

A) Overgeneralization
B) Jumping to conclusions
C) Disqualifying the positive
D) Labeling

All Are Correct - Choose The Response You Feel Is Most Important To Remember

Date ___/___/___ : S M T W Th F S

I feel:
(please circle)

because _____ because _____ because _____ because _____ because _____

Today I Am Grateful For

1. _____
2. _____
3. _____

What could help transform today into a remarkable day?

Reflective Writing

What are the benefits of recognizing my negative thinking patterns?

_____
_____
_____
_____
_____
_____
_____
_____

What is the purpose of recognizing negative thought patterns?

A) To eliminate all negative thoughts
B) To become more self-critical
C) To develop a more positive mindset
D) To ignore one's emotions

All Are Correct - Choose The Response You Feel Is Most Important To Remember

Date ___/___/___ : S M T W Th F S

I feel:
(please circle)

because _____ because _____ because _____ because _____ because _____

Today I Am Grateful For
1. _____
2. _____
3. _____

What could help transform today into a remarkable day?

Reflective Writing

What can I do to prevent my negative thoughts from impacting my behavior?

_____
_____
_____
_____
_____
_____
_____

Which cognitive distortion involves assuming that one knows what others are thinking without any evidence?

A) Mind reading
B) Personalization
C) Emotional reasoning
D) Magnification

All Are Correct - Choose The Response You Feel Is Most Important To Remember

Date ___/___/___ : S M T W Th F S

I feel:
(please circle)

😊	😁	😋	😟	😠
because	because	because	because	because
_____	_____	_____	_____	_____

Today I Am Grateful For
1. _____
2. _____
3. _____

What could help transform today into a remarkable day?

Reflective Writing
What can I do to help me focus on more positive thoughts?

_____
_____
_____
_____
_____
_____
_____

How can negative thought patterns impact one's daily life?

A) They can lead to a decrease in motivation
B) They can improve problem-solving skills
C) They can increase self-esteem
D) They can promote positive relationships

All Are Correct - Choose The Response You Feel Is Most Important To Remember

Date ___/___/___ : S M T W Th F S

I feel:
(please circle)

because _____ because _____ because _____ because _____ because _____

Today I Am Grateful For
1. _____
2. _____
3. _____

What could help transform today into a remarkable day?

Reflective Writing

How can I learn to recognize and respond to my own negative thinking?

_____
_____
_____
_____
_____
_____
_____

Which of the following is not an effective technique for managing negative thought patterns?

A) Mindful breathing
B) Rationalizing negative thoughts
C) Challenging negative thoughts
D) Distracting oneself from negative thoughts

All Are Correct - Choose The Response You Feel Is Most Important To Remember

Date ___ / ___ / ___ : S M T W Th F S

I feel:
(please circle)

because _____ because _____ because _____ because _____ because _____

Today I Am Grateful For

1. _____
2. _____
3. _____

What could help transform today into a remarkable day?

Reflective Writing

How can I use my support system to help me manage my negative thoughts?

_____
_____
_____
_____
_____
_____
_____

"I am a failure" is an example of which cognitive distortion?

A) Mind reading
B) Catastrophizing
C) Overgeneralization
D) Personalization

All Are Correct - Choose The Response You Feel Is Most Important To Remember

Date ___/___/___ : S M T W Th F S

I feel:
(please circle)

because _____ because _____ because _____ because _____ because _____

Today I Am Grateful For
1. _____
2. _____
3. _____

What could help transform today into a remarkable day?

Reflective Writing
How can I develop a plan of action to confront my negative thoughts?

_____
_____
_____
_____
_____
_____
_____

Which cognitive distortion involves blaming oneself for events or outcomes outside of one's control?

A) Emotional reasoning
B) Personalization
C) Magnification
D) Self-blame

All Are Correct - Choose The Response You Feel Is Most Important To Remember

Date ___ / ___ / ___ : S M T W Th F S

I feel:
(please circle)

😊 because _____
😁 because _____
😋 because _____
😟 because _____
😠 because _____

Today I Am Grateful For
1. _____
2. _____
3. _____

What could help transform today into a remarkable day?

Reflective Writing

How can I become more mindful of my negative thought patterns?

_____
_____
_____
_____
_____
_____
_____

Which of the following is not true about negative thought patterns?

A) They are always accurate
B) They can be based on past experiences
C) They can be influenced by one's emotions
D) They can be changed with practice and effort

All Are Correct - Choose The Response You Feel Is Most Important To Remember

Date ___/___/___ : S M T W Th F S

I feel:
(please circle)

😊 because _____
😁 because _____
😋 because _____
😟 because _____
😠 because _____

Today I Am Grateful For
1. _____
2. _____
3. _____

What could help transform today into a remarkable day?

Reflective Writing
What are the long-term benefits of recognizing and managing my negative thought patterns?

_____
_____
_____
_____
_____
_____
_____
_____

"I can't do anything right" is an example of which cognitive distortion?

A) All-or-nothing thinking
B) Mind reading
C) Disqualifying the positive
D) Labeling

All Are Correct - Choose The Response You Feel Is Most Important To Remember

Date ___/___/___ : S M T W Th F S

I feel:
(please circle)

😊	😄	😋	😟	😠
because	because	because	because	because
_____	_____	_____	_____	_____

Today I Am Grateful For
1. _____
2. _____
3. _____

What could help transform today into a remarkable day?

Reflective Writing
How can I create a safe space to process my negative thoughts?

_____
_____
_____
_____
_____
_____
_____
_____

Which of the following is not a common negative thought pattern?

A) Personalization
B) Discounting the positive
C) Catastrophizing
D) Rationalization

All Are Correct - Choose The Response You Feel Is Most Important To Remember

Date ___/___/___ : S M T W Th F S

I feel:
(please circle)

because _____ because _____ because _____ because _____ because _____

Today I Am Grateful For
1. _____
2. _____
3. _____

What could help transform today into a remarkable day?

Reflective Writing

How can I practice self-compassion when dealing with my negative thought patterns?

_____
_____
_____
_____
_____
_____
_____

Which of the following statements is an example of positive self-talk?

A) "I am a complete failure."
B) "I will never be able to do this."
C) "I am not good enough."
D) "I can learn from my mistakes and improve."

All Are Correct - Choose The Response You Feel Is Most Important To Remember

Date ___/___/___ : S M T W Th F S

I feel:
(please circle)

because because because because because
_____ _____ _____ _____ _____
_____ _____ _____ _____ _____

Today I Am Grateful For
1. _____
2. _____
3. _____

What could help transform today into a remarkable day?

Reflective Writing

What are some healthy habits I can practice to help me manage my negative thoughts?

_____
_____
_____
_____
_____
_____
_____

Brainspotting and cognitive restructuring are examples of which technique for managing negative thought patterns?

A) Mindfulness
B) Distraction
C) Rationalization
D) Psychotherapy

All Are Correct - Choose The Response You Feel Is Most Important To Remember

As we reach the final pages of this journey through "Positive Mindset," I want to extend my heartfelt thanks to you. Your commitment to exploring positivity and its transformative power is not only commendable but a testament to your desire for personal growth and a richer, more fulfilling life experience.

Remember, the journey towards a positive mindset is ongoing and ever-evolving. Each day presents new opportunities to apply these principles, to learn, and to grow. I encourage you to revisit these pages whenever you need a reminder of your incredible potential to foster positivity and resilience in the face of life's challenges.

As we part ways, I leave you with a quote that has been a guiding star in my journey: "The greatest discovery of any generation is that a human can alter his life by altering his attitude."

– William James.

Thank you for allowing me to be a part of your journey. May your path be filled with light, hope, and endless possibilities. Farewell, and may you carry the spirit of positivity with you, today and always.

With gratitude and best wishes,

Sensei Paul David

Reflective Writing

The End

As you close the pages of this mindfulness journal, remember that each word you've written is a step on your journey towards self-awareness and inner peace. Embrace the moments of clarity, the revelations, and even the uncertainties you've encountered along the way. Let this journal be a testament to your growth and a reminder that every day offers a new opportunity to be present, to observe, and to appreciate the simple wonders of life. Carry these lessons forward, and may your path be filled with mindful moments and serene reflections. Until we meet again in these pages, be gentle with yourself and stay anchored in the now.

Mindfulness isn't difficult, we just need to remember to do it.

Thank You!

If you found this book helpful, I would be grateful if you would **post an honest review on Amazon** so this book can reach other supportive readers like you!

All you need to do is digitally flip to the back and leave your review. Or visit amazon.com/author/senseipauldavid click the correct book cover and click on the blue link next to the yellow stars that say, "customer reviews."

As always...
It's a great day to be alive!

Get/Share Your FREE SSD Mental Health Chronicles at
www.senseiselfdevelopment.care

Check Out The SSD Chronicles Series CLICK HERE

Get/Share Your FREE All-Ages Mental Health eBook Now at
www.senseiselfdevelopment.com
Or CLICK HERE

senseiselfdevelopment.com

Click Another Book In The SSD
BOOK SERIES:
senseipublishing.com/SSD_SERIES
CLICK HERE

Join Our Publishing Journey!

If you would like to receive FREE BOOKS, please visit **www.senseipublishing.com**. Join our newsletter by entering your email address in the pop-up box

Follow Sensei Paul David on Amazon

CLICK THE LOGO BELOW

FREE BONUS!!!
Experience Over 25 FREE Engaging Guided Meditations!

Prized Skills & Practices for Adults & Kids. Help Restore Deep-Sleep, Lower Stress, Improve Posture, Navigate Uncertainty & More.

Download the Free Insight Timer App and click the link below:
http://insig.ht/sensei_paul

About Sensei Publishing

Sensei Publishing commits itself to helping people of all ages transform into better versions of themselves by providing high-quality and research-based self-development books with an emphasis on mental health and guided meditations. Sensei Publishing offers well-written e-books, audiobooks, paperbacks and online courses that simplify complicated but practical topics in line with its mission to inspire people towards positive transformation.

It's a great day to be alive!

About the Author

I create simple & transformative eBooks & Guided Meditations for Adults & Children proven to help navigate uncertainty, solve niche problems & bring families closer together.

I'm a former finance project manager, private pilot, jiu-jitsu instructor, musician & former University of Toronto Fitness Trainer. I prefer a science-based approach to focus on these & other areas in my life to stay humble & hungry to evolve. I hope you enjoy my work and I'd love to hear your feedback.

- It's a great day to be alive!

Sensei Paul David

Scan & Follow/Like/Subscribe: Facebook, Instagram, YouTube: @senseipublishing

Scan using your phone/iPad camera for Social Media
Visit us at www.senseipublishing.com and sign up for our newsletter to learn more about our exciting books and to experience our FREE Guided Meditations for Kids & Adults.

www.ingramcontent.com/pod-product-compliance
Lightning Source LLC
Chambersburg PA
CBHW072117070526
44585CB00016B/1487